How to draw
PEOPLE

**Written and Illustrated
by Barry Green**

Edited by Rebecca Flatman

Y0-CBF-673

FUNFAX™

First published in Great Britain by Funfax Ltd.,
an imprint of Dorling Kindersley Limited,
9 Henrietta Street, London WC2E 8PS
Funfax concept © Funfax Ltd.
Text and illustrations © 2000 Funfax Ltd.
© & TM The Media Merchants TV Co Ltd.

TOOLS AND MATERIALS

Paper

If you just want to practise your drawing skills, use cheap paper you won't mind throwing away if you don't like the results. You could use the plain back of scrap paper. If you are drawing a picture you want to keep, cartridge paper is good to use and can be bought in pads of different sizes.

Pencils

Start your drawings using a 2H or HB pencil. A 2H pencil makes hard, faint lines. It is good for planning out your picture, but the lines can be difficult to rub out if you press too hard.

Pens

Once you have your pencil drawing as you'd like it, outline it using a black fineliner pen then rub out all the pencil lines. If you are using felt-tip pens or paints to colour the picture in, it's best to use a waterproof black pen so that you won't smudge your lines.

Keep a small sketchbook and a pencil with you wherever you go, then you can draw interesting things you see – the more you draw, the better you'll become!

COLOURING IN

Coloured pencils
You can colour in your picture using coloured pencils. Start off lightly, then gradually darken the colour by pressing harder.

Felt-tip pens
These are good for colouring in, especially when you want nice bright colours.

Poster paints and acrylics
These paints are great for mixing together to create new colours. Tone down their colour by adding more water or mixing in white.

Tip

A good way of colouring in is to use felt-tip pens or paints as a base, then add shading with coloured pencils.

ART ATTACK

DRAWING THE HEAD AND FACE

Front view

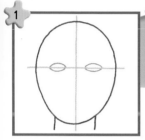

1 Start by drawing an egg shape for the head. Next, draw a line down the centre and a line across, about halfway down. Mark roughly where the eyes will be.

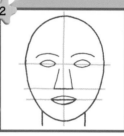

2 Add in another line halfway between the eye line and the chin. This is where the bottom of the nose goes. Below this, draw another line for the mouth.

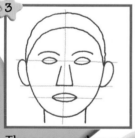

3 The ears are drawn between the eye line and the nose line. Indicate where the hair will grow.

4 Add details: eyebrows, eyelids, irises and pupils. Draw in some hair. Outline every detail with a black fineliner, then rub out your pencil markings. Colour in.

It's simple to draw a head looking up or down. Use the same head shape as before, just curve the guidelines as shown.

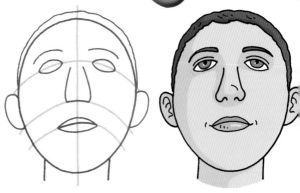

Curve the guidelines up to look up.

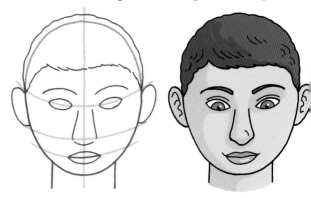

Curve the guidelines down to look down.

Side view

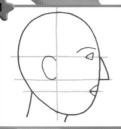

Draw an egg shape with one side flattened. Note where the point of the chin is. Position the features using the same guidelines as the front view face. The eye and lips are drawn in as triangular shapes. The ear is drawn behind a vertical centre line.

Add details. Show texture on the hair with pencil dashes. Give depth to the ears by adding curling lines. Use crease lines on the face to help show expression, round off the nose and give a nice pouting mouth! Notice where the iris and pupil go.

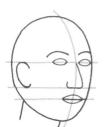

Three-quarter view

For this angle showing both eyes, use the same head shape and cross guidelines as the side view. The difference is the vertical line which curves around the head to show the position of the nose and mouth.

CARTOON FACES

Cartoon faces are easy to draw. Just draw an oval and then add in a cross. You can use the cross as a guideline for positioning the features.

Of course, you don't need to use any guidelines to draw cartoons like those shown below.

7

THE AGEING PROCESS

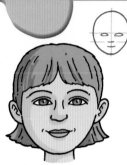

Baby/toddler
A baby or toddler's head is round and chubby. Draw the eyes below the guideline and make the nose small and cute.

Child
A child's face is slightly longer than a baby's, and the eyes are positioned just below the guideline. Make the nose slightly longer, too.

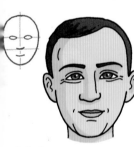

Adult
See page 4 for instructions on drawing an adult face.

Older person
Old people have sagging skin and wrinkles. Study their faces and add lines where you see them.

EXPRESSIONS

When drawing people, you can give them normal expressions or cartoon ones. Cartoon expressions tend to have simpler, more exaggerated features. Take a look at the examples below.

Normal   **Cartoon**

Happy
Big eyes and a contented smile make a happy expression.

Unhappy
See how miserable she looks with a downward-sloping mouth, eyes and eyebrows.

Angry

Draw a furrowed brow and narrowed eyes to give your character an angry look. Add a jeering mouth with bared, gritted teeth to put him in an even worse temper!

Surprised

Draw a small, rounded mouth to make a surprised expression. Oooh! The shape of the eyes is very important. They are wide open and the eyebrows go up!

Normal	Cartoon

Laughing

Draw closed eyes with creases at the sides and a beaming mouth. Add tears of laughter and a peeping tongue.

Frightened

Notice how the iris of the eye is smaller than the eye itself and the pupil is just a pin prick. The shape of the mouth is important in showing a frightened expression. It's open wide, showing teeth as it's gasping or screaming.

Tip

It's a good idea to pull faces in a mirror and copy them when you are trying to draw expressions.

DRAWING THE BODY

The important thing to remember about drawing people is 'proportion' – the size of body parts in relation to one another.

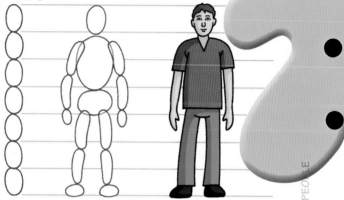

Front view

1. To get the body proportions right, draw 7 heads stacked up, then add lines as shown. The legs and the torso are both about three head lengths long.

2. Use sausage and egg shapes to draw a basic body.

3. Now draw over the guidelines and add details. Outline with a black fineliner and rub out the pencil marks.

Here's a side view.

BODY PROPORTIONS

Body proportions change with age.

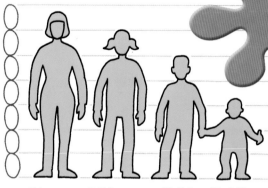

Woman   **Mid-teen**   **Child**   **Toddler**

To work out body proportions, draw a square with diagonal lines crossing in the centre. The cross shows approximately where the bottom of the torso will be.

The head should touch the top line and the feet the bottom. Outstretched arms will reach the sides of the square.

Sitting person
When a person is seated, they lose about two head lengths in height.

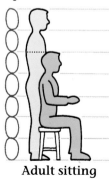

Adult sitting

13

CARTOON PEOPLE

Stick figures are the simplest way of drawing cartoon people.

1. First draw a stick figure, like so.

   Front   **Angle**   **Side**

2. Next, sketch sausage and egg shapes for the body, legs and so on.

3. Using the sausage and egg shapes as guides, draw clothes over them to complete the body shape.

Make your figures short and fat or tall and thin simply by changing the sizes of the sausages and eggs.

Like all cartoons, there are no rules to follow, so experiment with different shaped figures.

DRAWING HANDS

Hands can be difficult to draw, but with practice you'll be ready to tackle anything.

1. Again, start with some basic shapes joined together: sausages for fingers, a plate shape for the palm and an egg shape for the fleshy base of the thumb. Sketch curved lines to help you with the different finger lengths. The dots indicate where the joints are.

2. Draw over your guidelines. Add curved lines on the palm to show creases.

Side view
This picture shows how the fingers and thumb move. They can only bend forwards and not backwards.

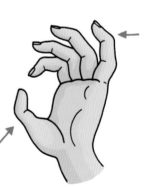

Practise sketching hands in different positions like those shown here:

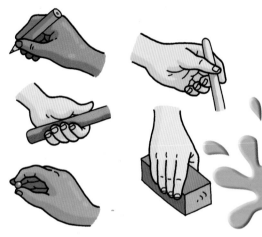

Cartoon hands are simpler to draw. Some cartoons show only three fingers, which makes it even easier!

DRAWING FEET

Feet are much easier to draw than hands.

Side view

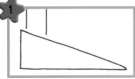

First draw a triangle to show the basic shape of the foot. Add two lines for the ankle.

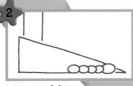

Next add in some egg shapes for the toes, starting with a big egg for the big toe and then four smaller ones.

Using the guidelines, draw in the foot shape. Add a curved line for the ankle bone.

Front view

First draw two triangles as shown. Sketch in each ankle.

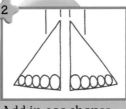

Add in egg shapes for the toes.

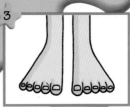

Round off the toes and smoothen out the lines. Draw in dainty toenails!

1

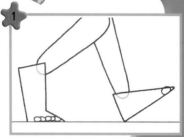

This picture shows how the feet look when walking. Start as before by breaking them down into simple shapes.

2

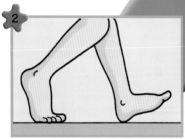

Next, draw over the guides. Look how there are more curves under the foot than above.

3

Feet are usually covered by shoes, so practise drawing these as well. Try sketching different styles.

Cartoon feet
Like hands, cartoon feet are easier to draw than lifelike ones. They can be as simple as you like.

DRAWING CLOTHES

Clothes are easy to draw. Ask a friend to dress up in different styles and practise sketching them. It could be quite a fashion show! Pay attention to details such as collars, cuffs and pockets. Try drawing hats, too.

Notice how stiff these drawings look. This is because there are no creases – you wouldn't be able to move wearing clothes like these!

Adding creases makes figures appear more natural, so draw them in where people move and bend – at joints such as the elbows, ankles, knees, at the waist, tops of the legs and under the arms.

Drawing wrinkles and curves adds movement and life to your drawings. When a figure moves, the creases change. Look when the girl twists how they twist to the side, too.

When she raises her arms, the material sags underneath.

DRAWING A MOVING BODY

The dots in this picture indicate the main moving joints of the body. Ask a friend to move in front of you, and practise sketching the different parts. See how far they move and bend.

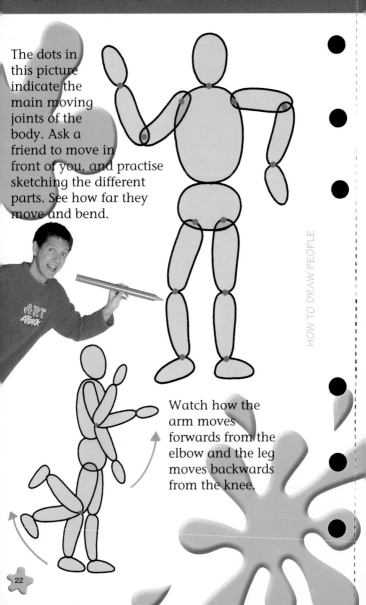

Watch how the arm moves forwards from the elbow and the leg moves backwards from the knee.

Practise drawing sausage and egg bodies in various positions, showing how the body bends at the joints. You could ask a friend to pose for you! Try drawing actions such as climbing, stretching and crawling. Add details when you are happy with the basic shape.

THE WALK

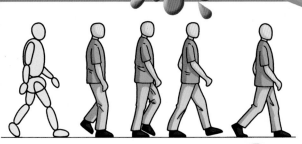

To draw people walking and running, first sketch their position using sausages and eggs, and then put in the details. When a person walks, one foot is always on the ground while the other moves forwards. Notice how the arms and legs move in opposite directions on the same side of the body. For example, the right arm swings forwards while the right leg moves backwards. The same thing happens when a person runs, but the arm and leg movements are both more exaggerated as the person increases the length of their stride to sprint ahead.

The main difference between the walk and the run is that both feet leave the ground when running. When you run quickly, you really are 'flying through the air'!

CARTOON MOVEMENTS

You can really exaggerate cartoon movements and go to town with details.

Cartoon walk
Look how big this character's strides are.

Cartoon run
Puffed out cheeks, a serious stare and gripped fists show how determined this person is to win the race. Add some movement lines to show a speedy character.

ACTION FIGURES

A great way to practise drawing moving figures is to copy from photographs you find in books and magazines. Sometimes tracing the picture first is a good idea, especially if the action is very complicated.

Over the next five pages there are instructions for drawing a selection of figures in action. Try those shown, then use what you have learned to sketch your own characters.

Ballerina

1. Draw a simple stick figure, adding dots where the joints are. Sketch lightly and rub out the pencil lines later.

2. Make the figure look more human by using sausage and egg shapes like those shown on page 12.

3. Now you can draw in the figure properly. Go over the outline with a black fineliner pen, then rub out the pencil marks. Colour in.

Surfer

Draw your figure in three stages, as you did for the ballerina. Take care to show his stance correctly. His outspread arms are held in front of him just enough to stop over-balancing. His legs are set firm on his surfboard. Show movement lines next to the board to suggest that it is cutting through the waves.

Footballer

This player is ready to strike the ball. Perfectly balanced, his arms are held out as he takes his foot back. With just a couple of lines you can emphasise his thigh muscles.

Tennis player

Show the player stretching to hit the ball. Her left leg is held out in front of her, feeling for the floor, while her right leg is stretched out behind.

Basketball player

This figure is swerving to his left, ready to dribble the ball. His body is twisted and his arm is stretched out to keep his balance and fend off attackers. Notice his outstretched fingers. A spread out hand is roughly equal to the size of a head in drawings.

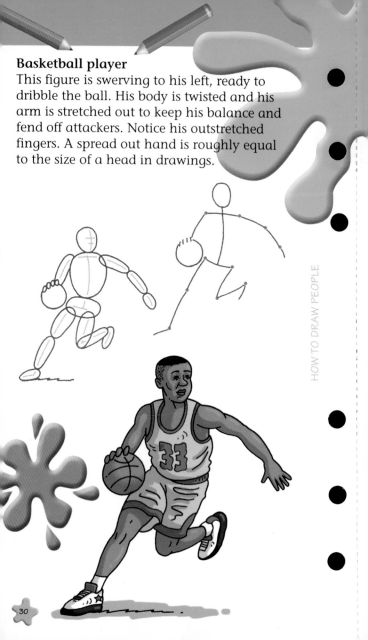

CARTOON ACTION

Really go over the top when showing cartoon characters in action. Start your pictures with simple stick figures and fill in details around these.

Look at the length of this player's arms and legs, and her huge feet! Draw movement lines to show the tennis ball bouncing off the ground.

This goalkeeper can't fail to stop the ball with his whopper gloves! The big gloves give a feeling of 'perspective' to the drawing. They look as if they are coming towards you.

Drawing cartoon people is great fun because you can make them do really silly things! Nobody could bend their limbs like this in real life...could they?

DRAWING CARICATURES

A caricature is a drawing of someone which exaggerates their features.

You really need to study the person you are drawing carefully. Pick out their most prominent features and make them bigger; make less important features smaller.

Your caricature doesn't have to be lifelike. Try drawing a cartoon version.